P9-CNI-760

Animal Camouflage

Hiding in a Rain Forest

Patricia Whitehouse

Heinemann Library
Chicago, Illinois

Designed by Cherylyn Bredemann
Printed and bound in the United States by Lake Book Manufacturing, Inc.
Photo research by Kathryn Creech

07 06 05 04
10 9 8 7 6 5 4 3 2

Library of Congress Cataloging-in-Publication Data
Whitehouse, Patricia, 1958-
    Hiding in a rain forest / Patricia Whitehouse.
        p. cm. -- (Animal camouflage)
    Summary: Describes life in a rain forest for animals and insects and how
    they use various forms of camouflage to survive, capture prey, and avoid predators.
        Includes bibliographical references (p.   ) and index.
        ISBN 1-40340-799-1 (HC), 1-40343-188-4 (Pbk)
        1. Rain forest animals--Juvenile literature. 2. Camouflage
    (Biology)--Juvenile literature. [1. Rain forest animals. 2. Camouflage
    (Biology) 3. Animal defenses.] I. Title. II. Series.
QL112 .W45 2003
591.47'2--dc21

                                                            2002010282

Acknowledgments
The author and publishers are grateful to the following for permission to reproduce copyright material: p. 4 Will & Deni McIntyre/Stone/Getty Images; p. 5 Steven Kaufman/Corbis; pp. 6, 7 Joe McDonald/Corbis; pp. 8, 9, 16, 30T Michael & Patricia Fogden/Corbis; p. 10 David M. Schleser/Nature's Images, Inc./Photo Researchers, Inc.; p. 11 Gail Shumway/Taxi/ Getty Images; p. 12 L. Bruce Kekule/Photo Researchers, Inc.; p. 13 George Holton/Photo Researchers, Inc.; pp. 14, 15 Michael Fogden/Animals Animals; p. 17 Mary Plage/Oxford Scientific Films; p. 18 Ralph A. Clevenger/Corbis; p. 19 Simon D. Pollard/Photo Researchers, Inc.; p. 20 Andew J. Martinex/Photo Researchers, Inc.; p. 21 Michael Lustbader/Photo Researchers, Inc.; p. 22 David A. Northcott/Corbis; p. 23 Jeff Lepore/Photo Researchers, Inc.; p. 24 Laura Sivell/Papilio/ Corbis; pp. 25, 30B Brian Kenney/Oxford Scientific Films; p. 26 Ray Coleman/Visuals Unlimited; p. 27 C. K. Lorenz/Photo Researchers, Inc.; p. 28 Gregory G. Dimijian/Photo Researchers, Inc.; p. 29 Gary Retherford/Photo Researchers, Inc.

Cover photography by Gail Shumway/Taxi/Getty Images.

Some words are shown in bold, **like this.** You can find out what they mean by looking in the glossary.

To learn about the glass frog on the cover, turn to page 11.

Contents

Hiding in a Rain Forest

Many animals live in the rain forest. Some rain forest animals are hard to see. They use **camouflage** to help them hide.

Some animals hide so they do not get eaten. Others hide from animals they want to catch and eat. There are many ways to hide. Red-lored Amazon parrots have **cryptic coloration.**

Hiding in a Tree

A gecko is hiding on this tree. The gecko's body is the same color as the tree. Animals that look like their **habitat** have **cryptic coloration**.

This gecko is a different color. It is easy to see.
Birds and other animals can find it and eat it.

Hiding on the Ground

Animals also hide on the ground. This bushmaster snake uses **cryptic coloration** to hide in the leaves. Its brown color helps it hide.

Here the ground is a different color. You can see the bushmaster. It can only hide if the ground is the same color as its **scales**.

Hiding in the Air

Some rain forest animals are **transparent** like the air. The clear-winged butterfly has wings you can see through. This makes the butterfly hard to see.

The glass frog is another transparent animal. Most of its body is clear. This helps the glass frog hide. It looks like the leaf it is sitting on.

Hiding by Looking Different

Some animals have color **patterns** that break up their shape. This is called **disruptive coloration.** The color pattern on this tapir makes it hard to see the whole animal.

This okapi has disruptive coloration on its legs.
The stripes break up the shape of the animal.
Predators have a hard time seeing the okapi.

Hiding by Staying Still

This vine snake has a long, thin body. It stays very still. This makes the snake look like a vine in the tree.

Sloths sleep in trees during the day. They stay very still. Sloths also have green **algae** growing on their fur. This makes them very hard to see.

Hiding to Hunt

The horned frog lives on the rain forest floor.
Its shape and color make it look like a leaf.
Prey do not see the frog until it is too late.

This jaguar is hiding in a tree. The spots on its fur make it look like the sun shining through the leaves. Prey might not notice the jaguar.

Pretending to Be Another Animal

These are weaver ants. When they bite, it hurts a lot. **Predators** stay away from weaver ants.

The Kerengga jumping spider **mimics** the weaver ant. Predators stay away because the spider looks like a weaver ant.

Hiding in a Flower

This crab spider has **cryptic coloration**. It is the same color as the yellow flower. This lets it hide on the flower.

But the crab spider cannot hide on this pink flower. It is easy to see. That is because the spider is not the same color as the flower.

Hiding in Plain Sight

Some forest animals do not hide. They **mimic** things that **predators** do not eat. This spiny leaf tail gecko looks like the tree it is resting on.

This is not a chewed-up leaf. It is a leaf **insect** that lives on rain forest plants. Here it looks like a leaf sitting on top of another leaf.

Pretending to Be Part of the Rain Forest

There is a butterfly in this picture. It looks like a dead leaf. It is called the dead leaf butterfly.

A treehopper is hiding on this plant. It is an **insect.** Its pointed wings **mimic** the shape of the plant's **thorns.** The treehopper uses mimicry to look like part of the plant.

Changing Colors

Chameleons can hide in many parts of the rain forest. They can change their colors. This chameleon looks like the branch it is resting on.

Now the chameleon is bright green. It has changed colors to look like a green branch.

Surprise!

This peanut head bug has a big head that looks like a peanut. The bug's head also looks like a lizard's head. **Predators** think they see a lizard and get scared.

Sometimes the peanut head bug opens its
wings. They have big **eyespots**. The spots
will surprise a predator, and it will run away.

Who Is Hiding Here?

What animals are hiding here?
What kind of **camouflage** do they have?

For the answer, turn to page 8.

For the answer, turn to page 25.

Glossary

alga (more than one are called algae)   kind of small plant

camouflage   use of color, shape, or pattern to hide

cryptic coloration   colors that make an animal look like the place where it lives

disruptive coloration   pattern of colors on an animal that makes it hard to see the whole animal

eyespots   spots shaped like animal eyes that scare predators away

habitat   place where an animal or plant lives

insect   animal with wings, six legs, three body parts, and a hard shell

mimic, mimicry   one animal looks and acts like a plant or another kind of animal

pattern   colors arranged in shapes

predator   animal that eats other animals

prey   animals that are eaten by other animals

scale   one of the small, stiff plates covering a snake's body

thorn   sharp point growing from a plant

transparent   can see through

More Books to Read

Arnosky, Jim. *I See Animals Hiding.* New York: Scholastic, Incorporated, 2000.

Galko, Francine. *Rain Forest Animals.* Chicago: Heinemann Library, 2002.

Kalman, Bobbie. *What Are Camouflage and Mimicry?* New York: Crabtree Publishing Company, 2001.

Index